Erstes Englisch
mit Billy Malone

Billy and his friends

Sich vorstellen • Sport • Den Weg finden

Von Christiane Grosskopf
Illustriert von Manfred Tophoven

TESSLOFF

Foreword

Vorwort

Herzlich willkommen in der Welt von Billy Malone!
Auf den nächsten Seiten begegnest du Billy, seiner Familie und seinem kleinen Hund Charly. Die Familie Malone begleitet dich bei deinen ersten Schritten in der englischen Sprache.
In lustigen Bildergeschichten und einfachen Sätzen erfährst du, was Billy mit seinen Freunden alles erlebt. Anhand von vielen leichten Aufgaben lernst du deine ersten englischen Wörter und festigst deinen Wortschatz.

Am besten lernst du Englisch, wenn du so viel wie möglich sprichst! Lass dir die englischen Wörter von jemandem vorlesen, der Englisch kann, damit du dir gleich die richtige Aussprache einprägst. Die Bildergeschichten kannst du dir auch im Internet auf **www.tessloff.com** anhören.

Damit man genau weiß, wie die Wörter ausgesprochen werden, gibt es die so genannte Lautschrift. Sie benutzt bestimmte Zeichen, die immer für einen ganz bestimmten Laut stehen. Im Vokabelverzeichnis am Ende des Heftes findest du hinter jedem englischen Wort auch die dazugehörige Lautschrift.

Dies sind die wichtigsten Zeichen:

- ɑː wie in lahm
- iː wie in Biene
- uː wie in Blume
- i wie in Baby
- ɪ wie in Kiste
- e wie in Bett
- æ ähnlich wie in Bär
- ʌ wie in Kamm
- ɒ wie in Motte
- ə wie in Mitte
- ʊ wie in Butter

- aɪ wie in Mai
- ɔɪ wie in Eule
- aʊ wie in Haus
- eə ähnlich wie in leer
- ɪə wie in Tier
- ɜː ähnlich wie in hört
- ʤ wie in Dschungel
- ʒ wie in Garage
- ŋ wie in Ring
- ʃ wie in Schlange
- ʧ wie in tschüss

- v wie in Vase
- z wie in Sonne
- s wie in Messer

Diese Laute gibt es nur in Englisch:

- θ wie in think
- ð wie in this
- w wie in water
- r wie in red
- eɪ wie in day
- əʊ wie in low

The Malones, Billy's family

Die Malones, Billys Familie

Herzlich willkommen bei den Malones!
Billy Malone ist 10 Jahre alt. Er wohnt mit seinen Eltern Mary und Peter und seinen beiden Schwestern Sally und Susan in einem hübschen Haus in einer kleinen Stadt in England.
Zur Familie gehören außerdem noch Oma Laura und Opa Joe, Onkel Tom und Tante Claire mit ihren beiden Kindern Peggy und Ron.
Ach ja, da fehlt ja noch einer: Natürlich gehört Charly auch zur Familie!
Charly ist der kleine Hund der Malones und Billys bester Freund.

Billy Malone

Charly, Billy's dog

Mary, Billy's mother

Peter, Billy's father

baby Susan

Sally, Billy's sister

Laura, Billy's grandmother

Joe, Billy's grandfather

Claire, Billy's aunt

Tom, Billy's uncle

Peggy, Billy's cousin

Ron, Billy's cousin

Stupid boy

Dummer Junge

Billy und Ron hatten einen normalen Tag in der Schule und sind auf dem Weg nach Hause. Da haben die beiden ein Erlebnis im Bus.

Schau dir die Bilder an. Weißt du, wie die Geschichte weitergeht? Versuche dann, die englischen Sätze zu lesen und zu verstehen.

Billy and Ron are getting on the bus to go home after school.

The bus is full today. Billy and Ron can't sit down.

"Ouch!" yells a girl. "You're standing on my foot, you stupid boy!"

"Oh, I'm very sorry, but I'm not stupid, my name is Billy."

A new family is moving into the house next to the Malones'.

Billy is sitting in the dining room. Someone is ringing at the door.

The new neighbours are saying hello.

"Hello, my name is Apala Khan," says the girl. Billy smiles and says: "My name is stupid boy!"

Billy's words

full – voll
today – heute
to sit down – sich setzen
to yell – schreien
to stand – stehen
foot – Fuß
I'm sorry. – Es tut mir leid.
my name is – ich heiße
to move in – einziehen
next to – neben
someone – jemand
to ring – klingeln
neighbour – Nachbar, Nachbarin
to smile – lächeln

Introducing oneself

Sich vorstellen

Wenn du jemanden triffst, den du noch nicht kennst, stellst du dich erst einmal vor. Du sagst, wie du heißt und wie alt du bist.

"My name is Billy Malone.
I'm 10 years old."

"My name is Ron Malone.
I'm 11 years old."

Auch Sally, Peggy, Opa Joe, Tante Claire und Peter Malone stellen sich vor:

Write down what they say.
Schreibe auf, was sie sagen.

Sally, 8

Peggy, 7

Joe, 60

Claire, 38

Peter, 37

Sally says: "My name is . . . . I'm . . . ."

Peggy says: . . . .

Joe says: . . . .

Claire says: . . . .

Peter says: . . . .

Hier siehst du verschiedene Länder in Europa.

Can you find the German names of the countries? Fill them in.
Findest du die Namen der Länder auf Deutsch? Trage sie ein.

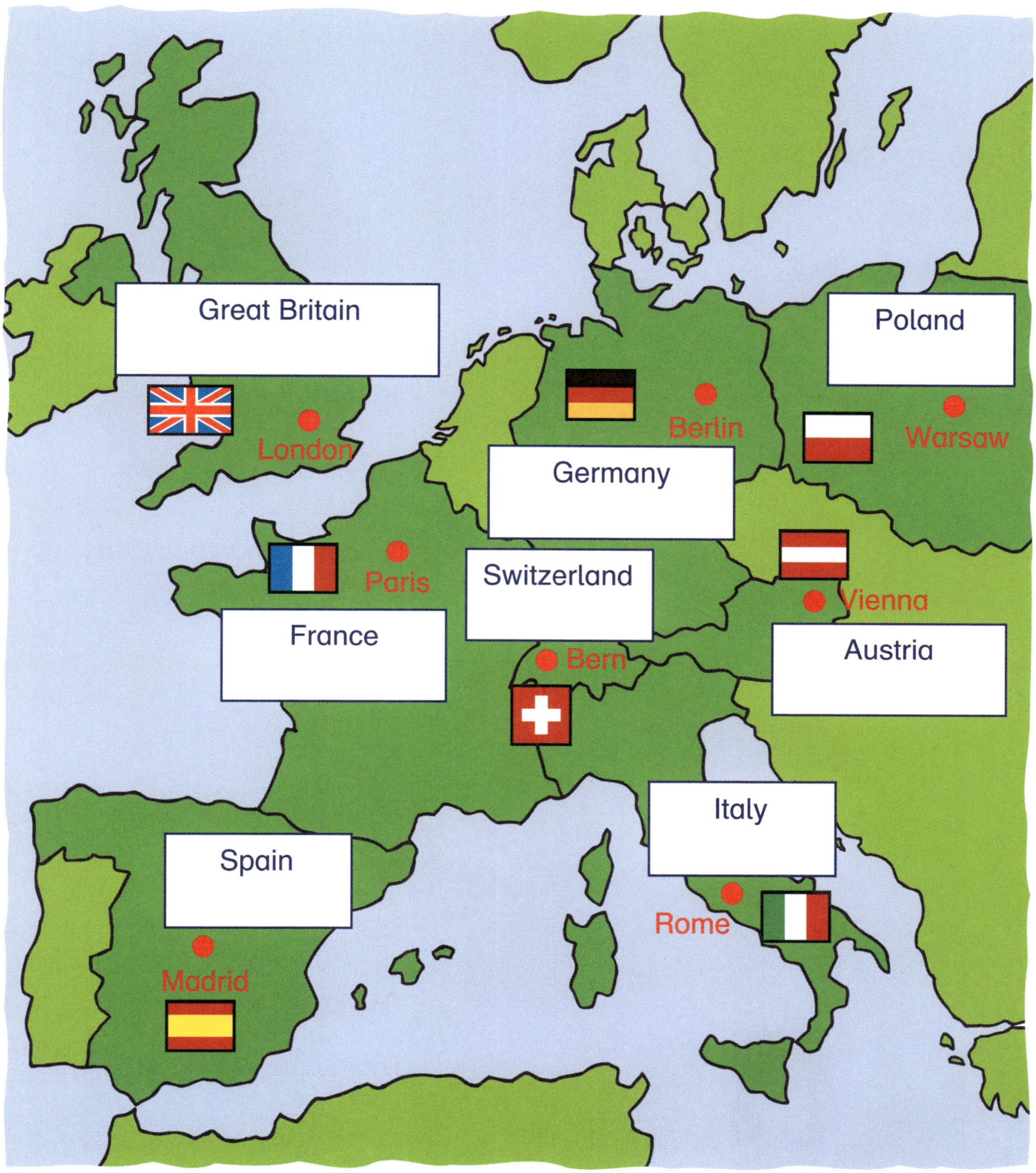

Großbritannien Spanien Frankreich Deutschland
Schweiz Österreich Italien Polen

Hier stellen sich Kinder aus verschiedenen Ländern in Europa vor.
Sie sagen, wie sie heißen und aus welchem Land sie kommen.

Complete the sentences: fill in the names of the countries.
Schreibe die Sätze zu Ende: Trage die Namen der Länder ein.

"Hello, my name is Billy.

I come from . . . ."

"Hello, my name is Linus.

I come from . . . ."

"Hello, my name is Max.

I come from . . . ."

"Hello, my name is Annika.

I come from . . . ."

Apala Khan, Billys neue Freundin aus Indien, stellt sich vor.

Connect the right parts of the sentences.
Verbinde die Satzteile, die zusammengehören.

My name is ...

... India.

I'm 10 ...

... Apala Khan.

I come from ...

... years old.

Nun kannst du sagen, wie du heißt, wie alt du bist und wo du herkommst.

Introduce yourself and draw a picture of yourself in the frame.
Stelle dich vor und male ein Bild von dir in den Rahmen.

. . . .

. . . .

. . . .

The football game

Das Fußballspiel

Billy, Ron und Charly spielen Fußball im Garten.

Schau dir die Bilder an. Weißt du, wie die Geschichte weitergeht?
Versuche dann, die englischen Sätze zu lesen und zu verstehen.

Billy, Ron and Charly are playing football in the Malones' garden.

Billy kicks the ball too hard. It flies over the fence!

The ball lands in front of Apala's feet.

Apala kicks the ball back. It lands in the goal! She plays football very well.

The next day Billy and Ron are playing against another football team.

Billy must shoot the penalty. He is proud.

Billy wants to score a goal and win the game.

Suddenly Billy looks at the goalkeeper. Oh dear! It's Apala!

Billy's words

too hard – zu fest
fence – Zaun
to land – landen
in front of – vor
goal – Tor
well – gut
the next day – am nächsten Tag
against – gegen
another – ein(e) andere(r,s)
penalty – Elfmeter
proud – stolz
to want – wollen
to score a goal – ein Tor schießen
to win – gewinnen
to look at – anschauen
goalkeeper – Torhüter

Sports
Sport

Hier siehst du viele Fußballwörter.

Match the football words to the right pictures. The colours will help you.
Ordne die Fußballwörter den richtigen Bildern zu. Die Farben helfen dir dabei.

goal penalty player football team

coach referee football game

Read the text and underline all the football words you can find.
Lies den Text und unterstreiche alle Fußballwörter, die du findest.

Hi, my name is Billy.

I play football every day in the garden.

I like my coach.

Ron plays in the same football team.

We practise shooting penalties.

Sometimes I score a goal.

Then I'm happy.

Die Bilder zur Geschichte oben sind in der falschen Reihenfolge.

Can you find the right order? Number the pictures.
Findest du die richtige Reihenfolge? Nummeriere die Bilder.

Hier siehst du, was Billy und seine Freunde mögen und was sie nicht gerne tun.

I like ...
Ich mag ...

I don't like ...
Ich mag nicht ...

Complete the sentences.
Ergänze die Sätze.

Billy likes football.

Billy doesn't like dancing.

Apala . . . . basketball.

Apala doesn't . . . . tennis.

Ron . . . . swimming.

Ron . . . . like gymnastics.

Die Kinder sagen, was sie mögen und was sie nicht gerne tun.

Draw lines.
Verbinde.

"I like swimming."

"I don't like football."

"I like tennis."

"I don't like basketball."

"I like dancing."

"I like gymnastics."

Jetzt bist du an der Reihe.

What do you like and not like?
Was machst du gerne und was magst du nicht?

I like . . . .

I don't like . . . .

The treasure hunt

Die Schatzsuche

Apala hat im Garten eine alte Flasche gefunden. Darin ist eine Karte, die zeigt, wo ein Schatz versteckt ist. Sie möchte mit Billy und Ron den Schatz suchen.

Schau dir die Bilder an. Weißt du, wie die Geschichte weitergeht? Versuche dann, die englischen Sätze zu lesen und zu verstehen.

"Look, I've got a bottle with a treasure map."

Apala, Billy and Ron are looking at the map.

The treasure is in the wood not far from the Malones'. "Let's go!"

The children are at the wood. "Let's walk 60 metres north."

"There's the oak tree. We must turn right there."

"Now we must walk 50 metres straight on and then turn left."

"Look, behind the big stone there's the treasure. How exciting!" says Ron.

Oh no! The chest is empty. There isn't any treasure!

Billy's words

bottle – Flasche
treasure – Schatz
map – Karte
not far – nicht weit
Let's go! – Lasst uns losgehen!
walk – gehen
north – nach Norden
to turn right – nach rechts gehen
straight on – geradeaus
to turn left – nach links gehen
behind – hinter
exciting – aufregend
chest – Kiste
empty – leer

Treasure hunt

Schatzsuche

Hier siehst du noch einmal die Wörter von der Schatzsuche.

treasure chest

bottle

oak tree

stone

map

turn right

turn left

go straight on

Can you fill in the missing letters?

Kannst du die fehlenden Buchstaben in die Wörter einsetzen?

st_n_ g_ str_ight o_ tu_n le_t m_p

tur_ righ_ oa_ tr_e bo_tle trea_ure che_t

Billy und Apala möchten ihre Freundin Sue besuchen. Sie waren beide noch nicht bei ihr zu Hause, aber sie haben eine Karte mit dem Weg.

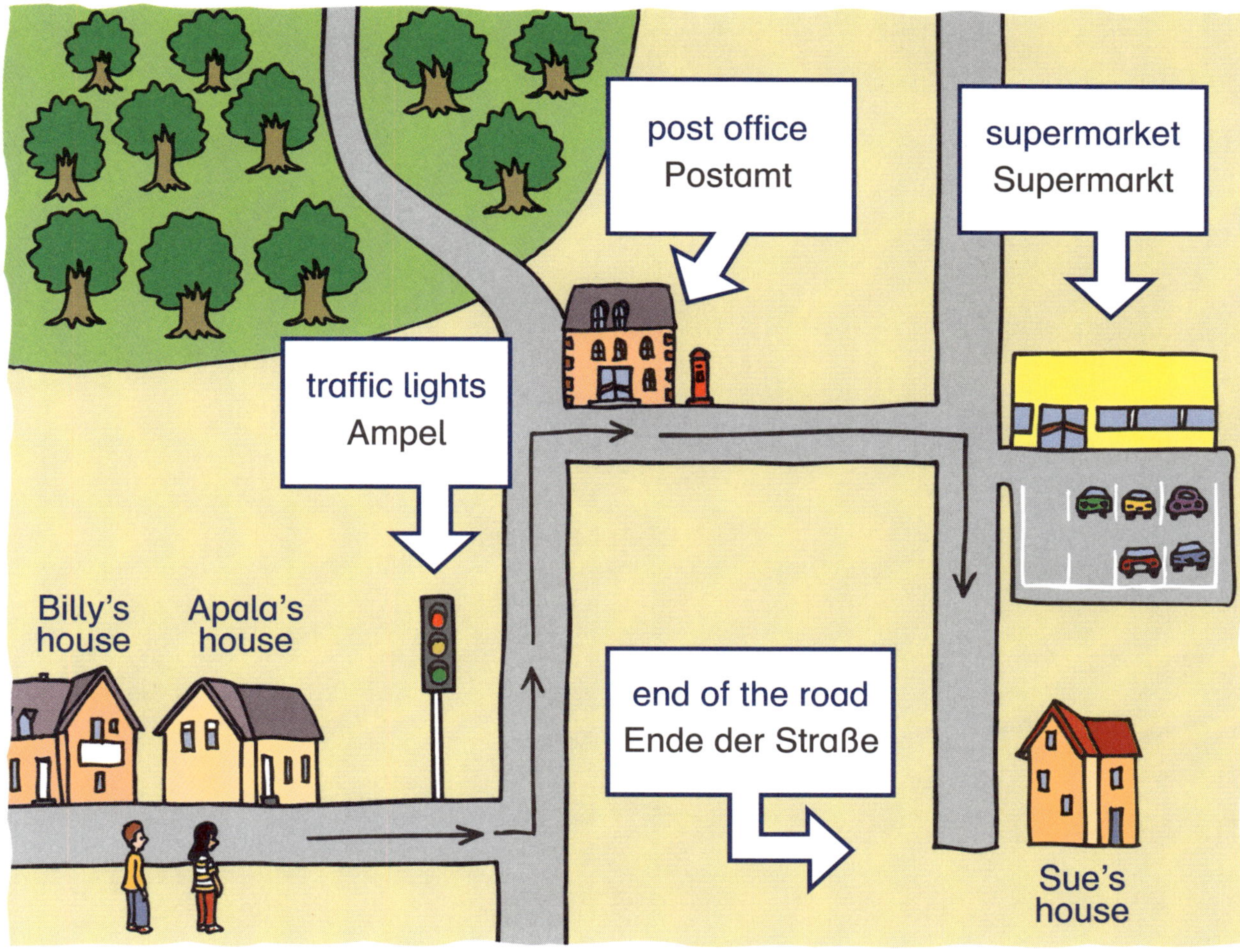

Look at the map and fill in the right direction.
Schau dir die Karte an und trage die Richtungen ein.

go straight on | turn left | turn right

We . . . . until we come to the traffic lights.

At the traffic lights we . . . .

Then we come to the post office. At the post office we . . . .

We can see the supermarket. At the supermarket we . . . . again.

Oh, look, there's Sue's house at the end of the road!

Hier siehst du Gegensätze. Kennst du schon alle Wörter auf Englisch?

Find the opposites and draw lines.
Finde das passende Gegenteil und verbinde.

The oak tree is big.

The chest is empty.

You must turn right.

The map is old.

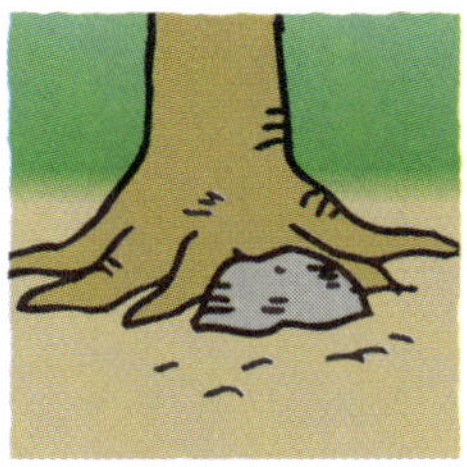
The stone is small.

The bag is full.

You must turn left.

The football is new.

Write down the opposites.
Schreibe die Gegensatz-Paare auf.

big – small ....

....

Vocabulary

Vokabeln

A

a [ə]	ein, eine
after ['ɑ:ftə]	nach
again [ə'gen]	wieder
against [ə'genst]	gegen
all [ɔ:l]	alle
and [ænd, ənd]	und
another [ə'nʌðə]	ein(e) andere(r,s)
at [æt, ət]	an, auf, bei, in
aunt [ɑ:nt]	Tante
Austria ['ɒstriə]	Österreich

B

baby ['beɪbi]	Baby
back [bæk]	zurück
bag [bæg]	Tüte, Tasche
ball [bɔ:l]	Ball
basketball ['bɑ:skɪtbɔ:l]	Basketball
to be [bi:]	sein
behind [bɪ'haɪnd]	hinter
Berlin [bɜ:'lɪn]	Berlin
Bern [bɜ:n]	Bern
big [bɪg]	groß
bottle ['bɒtl]	Flasche
boy [bɔɪ]	Junge
bus [bʌs]	Bus
but [bʌt, bət]	aber

C

can, can't [kæn], [kɑ:nt]	können, nicht können
chest [tʃest]	Kiste
children ['tʃɪldrən]	Kinder
coach [kəʊtʃ]	Trainer
colour ['kʌlə]	Farbe
to come [kʌm]	kommen
to complete [kəm'pli:t]	vervollständigen
to connect [kə'nekt]	verbinden
country ['kʌntri]	Land
cousin ['kʌzn]	Cousin, Cousine

D

to dance [dɑ:ns]	tanzen
day [deɪ]	Tag
dining room ['daɪnɪŋrʊm]	Esszimmer
direction [daɪ'rekʃən]	Richtung
do, don't [du:], [dəʊnt]	tun, nicht tun
dog [dɒg]	Hund
door [dɔ:]	Tür
to draw [drɔ:]	malen, zeichnen

E

empty ['empti]	leer
end [end]	Ende
every ['evri]	jede(r,s)
exciting [ɪk'saɪtiŋ]	aufregend

F

family ['fæmɪli]	Familie
far [fɑ:]	weit
father ['fɑ:ðə]	Vater
fence [fens]	Zaun
to fill in [ˌfɪl 'ɪn]	ausfüllen, eintragen
to find [faɪnd]	finden
to fly [flaɪ]	fliegen
foot, feet [fʊt], [fi:t]	Fuß, Füße
football ['fʊtbɔ:l]	Fußball
football game ['fʊtbɔ:l ˌgeɪm]	Fußballspiel
football team ['fʊtbɔ:l ˌti:m]	Fußballmannschaft
frame [freɪm]	Rahmen
France [frɑ:ns]	Frankreich
from [frɒm, frəm]	von, aus
full [fʊl]	voll

G

game [geɪm]	Spiel
garden ['gɑ:dn]	Garten
German ['dʒɜ:mən]	deutsch
Germany ['dʒɜ:məni]	Deutschland
to get on the bus [ˌget ɒn ðə 'bʌs]	in den Bus steigen
girl [gɜ:l]	Mädchen
to go [gəʊ]	gehen
to go home [ˌgəʊ 'həʊm]	nach Hause gehen
goal [gəʊl]	Tor
goalkeeper ['gəʊlˌki:pə]	Torhüter
grandfather ['grændˌfɑ:ðə]	Großvater
grandmother ['grændˌmʌðə]	Großmutter
Great Britain [ˌgreɪt'brɪtn]	Großbritannien
gymnastics [dʒɪm'næstɪks]	Turnen

H

hard [hɑːd]	fest, stark
happy ['hæpi]	glücklich
to have, to have got [hæv], [hæv 'gɒt]	haben
he [hiː]	er
hello [hel'əʊ]	hallo
to help [help]	helfen
hi [haɪ]	hallo
home [həʊm]	nach Hause
house [haʊs]	Haus
how [haʊ]	wie
How exciting! [ˌhaʊ ɪk'saɪtiŋ]	Wie aufregend!
hunt [hʌnt]	Jagd, Suche

I

I [aɪ]	ich
in [ɪn]	in
in front of [ɪn 'frʌnt əv]	vor
India ['ɪndiə]	Indien
into ['ɪntə, 'ɪntuː]	in (hinein)
to introduce oneself [ˌɪntrə'djuːs wʌn'self]	sich vorstellen
it [ɪt]	es
Italy ['itəli]	Italien

K

to kick [kɪk]	treten, kicken

L

to land [lænd]	landen
left [left]	links
Let's [lets]	Lass/Lasst uns
Let's go. [lets 'gəʊ]	Lass/Lasst uns gehen.
letter ['letə]	Buchstabe
to like [laɪk]	mögen
line [laɪn]	Linie
London ['lʌndən]	London
to look [lʊk]	schauen, gucken
Look! [lʊk]	Sieh mal!
to look at ['lʊk ət]	anschauen

M

Madrid [mə'drɪd]	Madrid
map [mæp]	Karte
to match [mætʃ]	zuordnen
metre ['miːtə]	Meter
missing ['mɪsɪŋ]	fehlend
mother ['mʌðə]	Mutter
to move [muːv]	umziehen
to move in [ˌmuːv 'ɪn]	einziehen
must [mʌst]	müssen
my [maɪ]	mein, meine

N

name [neɪm]	Name
neighbour ['neɪbə]	Nachbar(in)
new [njuː]	neu
the next [nekst]	der/die/das nächste
the next day [nekst 'deɪ]	am nächsten Tag
next door [nekst 'dɔː]	nebenan
next to ['nekst tuː]	neben
no [nəʊ]	nein, kein
north [nɔːθ]	(nach) Norden
not [nɒt]	nicht
not any [nɒt 'eni]	kein(e)
now [naʊ]	jetzt, nun
to number ['nʌmbə]	nummerieren

O

oak tree ['əʊktriː]	Eiche
Oh! [əʊ]	Oh!
Oh dear! [əʊ 'dɪə]	Oje!
old [əʊld]	alt
on [ɒn]	auf
oneself [wʌn'self]	sich selbst
opposite ['ɒpəzɪt]	Gegenteil
order ['ɔːdə]	Reihenfolge, Ordnung
Ouch! [aʊtʃ]	Aua!
over ['əʊvə]	über

P

Paris ['pærɪs]	Paris
part [pɑːt]	Teil
penalty ['penəlti]	Elfmeter
picture ['pɪktʃə]	Bild
to play [pleɪ]	spielen
to play football [ˌpleɪ 'fʊtbɔːl]	Fußball spielen
player ['pleɪə]	Spieler
Poland ['pəʊlənd]	Polen
post office ['pəʊstˌɒfɪs]	Postamt
to practise ['præktɪs]	üben
proud [praʊd]	stolz

R

to read	[ri:d]	lesen
referee	[ˌrefər'i:]	Schiedsrichter
right	[raɪt]	richtig, rechts
to ring	[rɪŋ]	klingeln
road	[rəʊd]	Straße
Rome	[rəʊm]	Rom

S

the same	[seɪm]	der/die/das gleiche
to say	[seɪ]	sagen
school	[sku:l]	Schule
to score a goal	[ˌskɔ: ə 'gəʊl]	ein Tor schießen
to see	[si:]	sehen
sentence	['sentəns]	Satz
she	[ʃi:]	sie
to shoot	[ʃu:t]	schießen
sister	['sɪstə]	Schwester
to sit	[sɪt]	sitzen
to sit down	[ˌsɪt 'daʊn]	sich setzen
small	[smɔ:l]	klein
to smile	[smaɪl]	lächeln
someone	['sʌmwʌn]	jemand
sometimes	['sʌmtaɪmz]	manchmal
Sorry!	['sɒri]	Entschuldigung!
I'm sorry!	[ˌaɪm 'sɒri]	Es tut mir Leid!
Spain	[speɪn]	Spanien
sports	[spɔ:ts]	Sport
to stand	[stænd]	stehen
stone	[stəʊn]	Stein
straight on	[ˌstreɪt 'ɒn]	geradeaus
stupid	['stju:pɪd]	dumm
suddenly	['sʌdənli]	plötzlich
supermarket	['su:pəˌmɑ:kɪt]	Supermarkt
to swim	[swɪm]	schwimmen
Switzerland	['swɪtsələnd]	Schweiz

T

team	[ti:m]	Mannschaft
tennis	['tenɪs]	Tennis
text	[tekst]	Text
the	[ðə, ði]	der, die, das
them	[ðem]	sie, ihnen
then	[ðen]	dann
there	[ðeə]	da, dort
today	[tə'deɪ]	heute
too	[tu:]	zu
too hard	[tu: 'hɑ:d]	zu fest
traffic lights	['træfɪkˌlaɪts]	Ampel
treasure	['treʒə]	Schatz
treasure chest	['treʒə ˌtʃest]	Schatztruhe
treasure hunt	['treʒə ˌhʌnt]	Schatzsuche
treasure map	['treʒə ˌmæp]	Schatzkarte
tree	[tri:]	Baum
to turn left	[ˌtɜ:n 'left]	nach links gehen
to turn right	[ˌtɜ:n 'raɪt]	nach rechts gehen

U

uncle	['ʌŋkl]	Onkel
to underline	[ˌʌndə'laɪn]	unterstreichen
until	[ʌn'tɪl]	bis

V

very	['veri]	sehr
Vienna	[vi'enə]	Wien

W

to walk	[wɔ:k]	gehen
to want	[wɒnt]	wollen
Warsaw	['wɔ:sɔ:]	Warschau
we	[wi:]	wir
well	[wel]	gut
what	[wɒt]	was, welche(r,s)
to win	[wɪn]	gewinnen
with	[wɪð]	mit
wood	[wʊd]	Wald
word	[wɜ:d]	Wort
to write	[raɪt]	schreiben
to write down	[ˌraɪt 'daʊn]	aufschreiben

Y

year	[jɪə]	Jahr
to yell	[jel]	schreien
you	[ju:]	du, ihr, Sie
yourself	[jɔ:'self]	dir/dich selbst

Solutions

Lösungen

Seite 6

"My name is Sally Malone.
I'm 8 years old."

"My name is Peggy Malone.
I'm 7 years old."

"My name is Joe Malone.
I'm 60 years old."

"My name is Claire Malone.
I'm 38 years old."

"My name is Peter Malone.
I'm 37 years old."

Seite 7

Great Britain – Großbritannien

Poland – Polen

Germany – Deutschland

France – Frankreich

Switzerland – Schweiz

Austria – Österreich

Italy – Italien

Spain – Spanien

Seite 8

"Hello, my name is Billy.
I come from Great Britain."

"Hello, my name is Linus.
I come from Germany."

"Hello, my name is Max.
I come from Austria."

"Hello, my name is Annika.
I come from Switzerland."

Seite 9

My name is Apala Khan.
I'm 10 years old.
I come from India.

My name is ...
I'm ... years old.
I come from ...

Seite 12

Tor – goal

Schiedsrichter – referee

Spieler – player

Fußballmannschaft – football-team

Fußball – football

Elfmeter – penalty

Trainer – coach

Spiel – game

Seite 13

Hi, my name is Billy.

I play football every day in the garden.

I like my coach.

Ron plays in the same football team.

We practise shooting penalties.

Sometimes I score a goal.

Then I'm happy.

2 – 5 – 1 – 4 – 3

Seite 14

Apala likes basketball.
Apala doesn't like tennis.

Ron likes swimming.
Ron doesn't like gymnastics.

Seite 15

"I like swimming.":
Bild unten rechts

"I don't like football.":
Bild Mitte links

"I like tennis.":
Bild oben rechts

"I don't like basketball.":
Bild unten links

"I like dancing.":
Bild oben links

"I like gymnastics.":
Bild Mitte rechts

Seite 18

stone, go straight on, turn left, map, turn right, oak tree, bottle, treasure chest

Seite 19

We go straight on until we come to the traffic lights.

At the traffic lights we turn left.

Then we come to the post office.
At the post office we turn right.

We can see the supermarket.
At the supermarket we turn right again.

Oh, look, there's Sue's house at the end of the road!

Seite 20

The chest is empty. – The bag is full.

You must turn right. – You must turn left.

The map is old. – The football is new.

empty – full

right – left

old – new